Photo Credit: Michelle Frankfurter

Robin Morgan has published over twenty books, including six poetry collections. Her first, *Monster*, caused an international furor; her TED Talk reading of *Dark Matter* poems has garnered over one million downloads. She is a recipient of the U.S. National Endowment for the Arts Prize in Poetry and her work has been widely translated. An activist in the global Women's Movement for decades, recognised as a leading architect of U.S. feminism, and a former Editor-in-Chief of *MS.* magazine, she co-founded The Sisterhood Is Global Institute with Simone de Beauvoir and co-founded The Women's Media Center with Jane Fonda and Gloria Steinem.

www.RobinMorgan.net
www.facebook.com/TheRobinMorgan/
Twitter @TheRobinMorgan

Also by Robin Morgan

Poetry
A Hot January: Poems 1996–1999
Upstairs in the Garden: Selected and New Poems
Depth Perception
Death Benefits
Lady of the Beasts
Monster

Fiction
The Burning Time
Dry Your Smile
The Mer Child

Nonfiction
Fighting Words: A Toolkit for Combating the Religious Right
Saturday's Child: A Memoir
The Word of A Woman: Essays
The Demon Lover: The Roots of Terrorism
A Woman's Creed
The Anatomy of Freedom
Going Too Far

Anthologies (compiled, edited, and introduced)
Sisterhood Is Forever
Sisterhood Is Global
Sisterhood Is Powerful
The New Woman (co-ed.)

DARK MATTER

New Poems

ROBIN MORGAN

SPINIFEX

First published by Spinifex Press, 2018

Spinifex Press Pty Ltd
PO Box 5270, North Geelong, Victoria 3215
PO Box 105, Mission Beach, Queensland 4852
Australia
women@spinifexpress.com.au
www.spinifexpress.com.au

Acknowledgements

Some of these poems have previously appeared in the following publications and contexts:

Thirteen of these poems were published as a special feature in the June 2014 issue of *Poesia* (Milan), in Italian translation by Maria Nadotti with Cristina Aziati, as facing pages with the original English: "Barbarina's Cavatina," "The New Old Woman," "Bioluminescence," "Hunger," "Content Content" (included here as "Final Proof"), "A Worm of Robins," "Disclosure," "Compass," "Grey Matter," "No Signs of Struggle," "At the Edge of the Wheatfield," "Invitation," and "The Magician and the Magician's Assistant."

Four of these poems—"No Signs of Struggle," "On Donating My Brain to Science" (part II of "Grey Matter"), "The Ghost Light," and "This Dark Hour"—were read aloud as a featured TED Talk by the poet in May 2015, and were subsequently translated by request into 24 languages with to date over one million distinct views online.

An earlier version of "The Excavation" first appeared in print in *The Hudson Review*, Spring 2017 issue.

"The Ghost Light" was first published in *Poetry*, September 2017.

"Disclosure," "Compass," "Giants at the Corner Table," and "The Magician and the Magician's Assistant" were published in *Live Encounters: Lesbian Poets and Writers*, February 2018.

Cover design: Deb Snibson
Typesetting: Helen Christie
Typeset in Fairfield Light
Printed in the US

Paperback   9781925581430
ePub   9781925581461
Adobe PDF   9781925581447
Kindle   9781925581454

A catalogue record for this book is available from the National Library of Australia

For Blake and Janita

Contents

I. **Doing the Blood Work**
The Magician and The Magician's Assistant   1
Barbarina's Cavatina   2
Doing the Blood Work   3
   1. The Inheritance
   2. Not by Halves
The Fossil of A Young Woman   5
Ice Dancing   6
The Contortionists   9
Kigali, 1994   10
Compass   12

II. **The New Old Woman**
The New Old Woman   15
Hunger   17
Bioluminescence   18
Transmitting Gravity   19
Giants at the Corner Table   21
Needlework   23
Meteor Shower   25
Final Proof   31

III. **Grey Matter**
No Signs of Struggle   35
Grey Matter   37
   1. Movement Disorder
   2. On Donating My Brain to Science
   3. Images
Uniquely Human   40
Looking on the Bright Side   43
At The Edge of The Wheatfield   45

The Ghost Light   48
Bodily Knowledge   50
Invitation   52

IV. Dark Matter
    A Worm of Robins   57
    The Young Artists at Rockwood Music Hall   58
    Trying to Write A Poem At the Very Last Minute 60
    The Excavation   62
    Disclosure   67
    Reading the Bones   69
    This Dark Hour   72
    Disappear   73

DARK
MATTER

I.
Doing the Blood Work

The Magician and The Magician's Assistant

I've had me up my sleeve
I've pulled me from my hat
I've planted myself in the audience
as the patsy I dare to decipher my tricks—
safe I can never see through me.

The Magician and The Magician's Assistant—
I've been both for so long.
Introducing myself with a smile and a flair
and a white-gloved bow to applause. Then
making myself disappear.

Well, I can tell you I'm done
dodging knives flung at my head,
done being folded into cramped crates,
sawed into pieces again and again. I am done,
in short, with being The Magician's Assistant.

From here on in, I need no assistant,
no props, no stage, no audience.
From here on in, all that's left
is The Magician.
Or so I thought.

That was before I could comprehend
that I'm also done flinging the knives,
bowing, smiling, drowning
in chains upside down, done
holding my breath.

So nothing is left to perform now.
Sorry to disappoint.
I have my own bare hands full
grasping how
from here on in, all that's left is the magic.

Barbarina's Cavatina

Such anguish over a lost pin,
a common though useful fastener.
Surely a petty tragedy,
humorous even, hardly
worthy of the minor key.

Yet Mozart knew it as a common grief,
the loss of something ordinary—a father's kiss,
an unsent letter—something small
we search for, as if that might have held
the fragments of a life together, after all.

Doing the Blood Work

1. The Inheritance

Most family truths lie audibly unsaid
and I, a child who probed to no avail,
learned any who could answer me were dead.

For years, through dimming hope lit by bright dread,
I staggered alone along abandoned trails,
till I ceased caring. Then of course, news came. Unsaid

though, any testament except half-lies, spoon fed
by two half-brothers, new-found, who wore my smile.
I cared again. Yet they were true sons of our undead

father, who'd rutted my mother in a ghostly bed.
A secret child, to father and sons, required denial
of what they dared not know. Still, truth's unsaid

the whole world over; everyone has bled
their part; how else but numb can the heart prevail?
So my twice-lost half-blood kin claimed, dead

to untold truths from which lifelong they'd fled.
Many die out their days this way and will
their children's truths in turn to lie unsaid.
But I'm done caring who lies living, who lies dead.

2. Not By Halves

Do two half brothers make one whole?
I thought they might. I thought
this meeting, late in life, was like a minor miracle.
I'd learn so many things! But not what I expected.

One brother, middle child, stalks his life
famished for the father he disappointed
despite all he tried. So he beat ploughshares
into swords, grew sons who are religious warriors.

The other, the youngest, our father's favorite,
reenacts the tearless manhood he'd learned
so well, emotions stored inside a citadel despite
his music's artistry that blurred my seeing him for tears.

Civilized, intelligent, educated men, neither
was prepared for the elder sister whose existence
they'd discovered decades earlier and had
pursued but briefly, fearful and half-hearted.

Our father dead now, everyone spoke earnestly
at first, through bad translation. But his ghost rose
and walked, reminding his sons they'd been taught
secrets, half truths, denials, rationales. It took some

years to raise my old scars by these new means,
but in good time, livid, the wounds ran fresh.
It's necessary to relearn trust
before one can relearn betrayal.

The distance with the older already formal,
that fracture was less painful. The younger, a performer,
promised more than he decided to deliver, though.
His children we can leave in charitable silence.

It's calmer now they're gone
and I'm an only child again.
Their absence is as normal as my father's was.
Now all is wept and done,

stains of our personal blood libel rinsed
off by a family history engraved on water.
They were always their father's sons,
I was always my mother's daughter.

The Fossil of A Young Woman

The structure of every organic being is related in the most essential manner to that of all other organic beings with which it comes into competition, from which it has to escape, or on which it preys.
—CHARLES DARWIN, 1859

Each morning she strokes multicolor
mascara on her lashes and explores
her closet: a consciousness rummaging among
moods for something to wear.
She has no clue so far that she is the
"ashcan edition" of a comic book:

the only copy ever printed. Yet
she suspects she suffers a different metabolism
of mind. Collectors are after her, but she eludes
their cabinets. She is waiting for something
to begin: an age, a self, a melody. Meanwhile,
she sleeps, dreaming she's fallen awake.

Approximately 120 elements compose
her. Her atoms number in the billions.
She is 95 percent hydrogen, carbon,
nitrogen, oxygen,
phosphorus, calcium.
She has no idea who she is.

One day she will look back and wince—not with regret,
but scorn. She will have chosen evolution. Meanwhile,
she watches the murders through clouded eyes.
Those who claim to love her cry *Let us prey!*
She flees, but learns to turn when cornered,
teeth bared, snarling.

Ice Dancing

for KB and CB

All those decades of pairs competition,
lifts betrayed to bruised landings, pivots,
flips backsliding as your partner lunges,
loops razoring ice so cross-hatched neither
skater knows whose blade has the inside edge.
Not that it matters, since compulsory programs
usually end in the pair spin named Death Spiral.
A partner seems a given, since only pairs

can qualify: solo has no standing
in the trials. It isn't judged a sport
unless you give up dancing and settle for making
figures. My partners were all talented.
The last one was a pro, a real athlete
I had mistaken for an artist: my fault.
After that—though coaches, judges, fans
claim no one switches specialty in mid-

career—I changed. Perhaps I lack the patience
for pairs. Yet I admire those who persist
in daily practice. They deserve medals of real gold.
Me, I left the costumes, rules, requirements,
Tchaikovsky crescendos, kiss-and-cry corners.
But not ice. I never left the ice.
I took to dancing in the wild: frozen
country ponds, backwater pools. No time

clocks but my own, or nightfall, or spring thaw;
snowhush muffle my sole music, space
to the shore all mine to glide, sailing the mast
my spine has always been, slicing the wind.
A rare passerby might watch awhile—
not unwelcome, not invited, and not
missed. Once or twice I spied another
dancer. Each time we bowed, and kept our distance.

Now, when the seasons change, I go farther
north. Risk is assumed. Still, after
the first spill through thin ice, I took more pains
to be less careful. I have learned some things.
How useless it is to thrash and scream. How what
you wear—for warmth, you think—can weigh you down.
How rage will buoy you up when hope cannot:
driving your fist with a power that shatters the pearl-

blue ceiling into powdered-sugar flakes.
Sometimes I wonder whether I dance the ice
to fly upon it or to seek what currents
swirl beneath. Each plunge I relearn how
to bear this element, how to swim
numb liquid ice, locate the broken place above
by following light fracturing in prisms
radiant from where entry and exit are the same,

then to erupt gasping, clawing the pale sun. I hold
such lessons in my lungs now, unsure how long
it will be this time, unsure how long it's been
since I was up there gathering speed on a take-off
edge ... but it was young ice,
only early winter ice. So after the leap
and landing, came the
knowledge.

Then crust crack, trap-door drop, slurry churning
a dream motion universe where only heartboom
ever really marks the time, where each
of us—whether we think we stand on solid ground
or recognize we dance on ice—
drifts solo past rising chains of crystal roe,
breath silvering up to bounce in laughter
bubbles against a milkglass melting sky.

The Contortionists

for RL

They
put their noses to the
grindstone, shoulders
to the wheel, ears to the
ground, backs to the wind
eyes on the prize

They
put their time in,
money on it
muscle to it
hearts in it
eyes on the prize

They
put all of their eggs in one
of their baskets, put in their oars,
put their feet on the floor, their minds
over matter, their hearts in their mouths
eyes on the prize

They
glimpse what they've missed when
it's done, though: the view rushing by
blurred then forgotten, theirs all along
each instant of the nonrenewable now
its own surprise

We
put away our regrets, then,
deny the indifference of azaleas,
ignore what hides in intricate sight
from the contortions ambition devises,
failing to see the abundance of prizes.

Kigali, 1994

for IR

The clipping is yellow, brittle, but still
you can read it: how Hutu militiamen slaughtered
the patients—all 750 of them—at the mental facility.
They threw grenades over the wall, remembers
a nurse. She says "The patients did not understand
what was happening. They started to wander
around singing, with their hands in the air."

Another recalls that the mobs who came
bearing their instruments of murder swept
through churches where Tutsis hid sweating,
through villages, suburbs, cities, killing
in schools, homes, parishes, fields. "They were
like bureaucrats," one woman remembers, "They
started each morning at 7, and they quit at 5."

After a hard day's murders, they would return
to their homes in the hills, singing, carrying spoils
stolen from victims, like the teenage girl thrown into a hole
with several dead children. Villagers heard
her cries and passed her down water. Then the mayor
ordered the hole to be covered, and villagers covered the hole.
The people who'd passed her down water covered the hole.

This is old news now, yellow as cowardice, brittle
as sanity. Rwanda's undergoing reconstruction,
the killing's moved on. There's always a massacre
playing somewhere; if you miss the matinée
you can catch the evening show, or get it on demand.
There are reruns, too, complete
with commentary, analysts, perspective.

Young, I vowed to stop it or live trying. Old now,
skin yellowing, bones brittle, simply by staying alive
in some way I joined those who returned home
singing, carrying spoils stolen from others' suffering:
subject matter for a poem. I did not understand
what was happening. So I started to wander
around, singing, like this, with my hands in the air.

Compass

There's a lost south in me, a place where joy,
though costly, was a common middle name.
Tomorrow, there, had elsewhere stayed today,
solstices changed places, nothing was the same.
There at the world's edge, the antipodes,
with all the stars and seasons rearranged,
earth's axis seemed to shift and gravity's
force drew me in. My latitudes since then have changed.
A lost love, like a phantom limb, gestures
emptily, making itself felt through pain.
So ached this south in me for many years.
But the world is round, and the lost self was regained
once, seeking my own south, I ventured forth
in due course, with due diligence, due north.

II.
The New Old Woman

The New Old Woman

for JSF

> *Energy can be changed from one form to another,*
> *but cannot be created or destroyed.*
> —THE FIRST LAW OF THERMODYNAMICS

The old woman is never wholly who she thinks she is
because she's also always everyone she ever was—
though never quite the woman others are sure they knew.

The face she bares today is one the world has never seen:
a face till now only old women suspected
in one another, recognizing those sweet secret selves

we've relished while others winced: youth's fleshy tissue
stripped to bone arcs clean as driftwood, shadows unfurling
unafraid of depth pooled in unshallow sockets, surfaces

of skin once tight as a drum requiring blows
to make its music now free to comprehend at last
what the brain knew all along: intelligence grows in furrows.

See how these eyes choreograph desire assumed dead
though alive, erotic, furious. Watch this wry mouth ply
its uncensored truths and seek out more, still curious. See

this body stand, dance, lie through pain now tolerable that once
could stop her cold. See her respect her hungers, laugh out loud
at the notion she might settle for less than she deserves.

Watch her feed others with her power, art, time, love.
See her no longer apologize for her impatience
with all things stupid, cruel, unnecessary.

Not to deny the darkness that bore her—or that
through which she journeys, purposeful, her thirst to be useful
craving to slake the thirst of those who suffer the dark unseen.

And never to deny the other, gathering darkness beyond
a horizon against which all this glows. Rather, to understand
just who it is we are, and who becoming:

Fireflies cluster in the shadiest part of a garden,
in the slate dusk greying under the trees. They shun
the twilight that clings, gaudy, to the sunset.

They know the darker it gets, the greater the contrast
for their scintillescence, the more they can recognize
each other's fire. So is the old woman now wholly

who she knows she is, because she's also everyone
she ever was—with a few last brightening selves yet to gleam
more luminous as the night comes on.

Hunger

The old woman realizes
that in her time she's fed

at least eight cats,

two dogs,

approximately 40 goats,

six cows and three calves,

three sheep and four chickens,

four swans, six ducks, two geese,

and cardinals   bluejays   house sparrows
barn sparrows   english sparrows   plain
finches   golden finches   mourning doves
titmouses   robins   downy woodpeckers
even starlings   a parrot   a parakeet
even pigeons it must be confessed

plus

a forest-worth of plants,

breakfast and lunch and dinner guests,

(brunch, too, and suppers and teas and snacks)

far too many men in her youth, and

one small human being with her body's milk.

All this she chose to do, wanting to feed the world.

But nothing ever feels fed.
Only the old woman is finally sated.

Bioluminescence

Young, she smiled "Thank you"
when they marveled how much she
thought like a man, and later
didn't look her age, when they spoke
admiringly of her high tolerance for pain.

Mature, she tried her best—one of the better
bests—but simply wasn't brave or smart
enough to let herself free. She surrendered to hope.
She spent her days and her nights toward building
a world where no one—no one—ever dies in vain.

Now, busy with this new learning
how to totter and decay, how to settle in a body
alien though familiar, the old woman concedes
there are some things she cannot fix—
though she doesn't always know what they are, yet.

But she's free to eat popcorn and blueberries
for dinner, munching while mulling a poem's
worth of words. See her in her kitchen,
in her nightgown, at 3 AM?
A TV voice drifting from the other room

explains how life forms in the deepest ocean dark
generate their own light. There it is again, that light.
See her? She's conjugating *I am, you are, each of us is*
a glowing fragment—eternally perishing—of all
that exists. So, in her nightgown, the old woman

dances alone in her kitchen, and, on a whim,
practices juggling oranges at 3 AM.
Why?
Because everyone dies
in vain.

Transmitting Gravity

Pressure.
Pressure wants.

The boiling metal core of this planet wants,
while gravity balances its orbit and we
swarm its surface running, running out
of time out of mind.

Already, palm trees bask
where pines once sighed.

Weak force, strong force, one force only
able to re-collect everything still being one thing
afloat in its own interior sea before most of us
came to cling, broken, to the sands of bleak atolls
floating swift currents of despair.

Pressure.
We are drawing together

while rushing apart.
Why do individuals imitate each other? Not
only humans. Something deeper. All
the wildebeast in the Serengeti ovulate
the same week. Something that cries into
airless space,

Am   I   alone?
Is   anything   there?

Why do species imitate each other?
The hummingbird moth. The stone-shaped cactus.
Mint plants that taste of chocolate, geraniums
that smell like oranges. A limited palette?
Or the inability to use limitlessness? Or the pressure
to repeat something repeat different
from the same? Mind out of time.
What if gravity is defined
by longing?

Insufficient eternity to make enough poems,
enough particles of light to live along the dark
ribbons of matter. Scientists in Darmstadt
have stopped the fastest thing in the universe, light,
dead still, for one minute, inside a crystal.
Why
would they want to do that:
stop light?

Pressure.

Time out of mind.

What if gravity is defined

by patience?

Giants at the Corner Table

for SBL, JE, GS, and MT

New at being old, they marvel at it:
aches in places they never knew they had,
memory lapses, the unrecognizable
stooped image scurrying past
the shop window reflection.
They laugh about it wryly, comparing notes.

These particular new old women have been friends
and colleagues for 40 years. For 30 of those years,
once jobs took them on differing paths,
all five have met for dinner every month
no matter what other social occasions
they might also share. Close to 400 dinners.

They have marched and picketed, lobbied,
fundraised, sat in; still do. And seen each other through
childbirths, weddings, divorce, hospitals, book parties,
funerals, birthdays. They bring small presents
back from trips, share running jokes. They've learned
to tolerate in one another what they could not love.

And they have rituals:
the white wine drinker who likes a separate glass of ice;
the one who brightens when ordering dessert;
the one who can't stand cinnamon in her cappuccino;
the one who would dine at 5 PM if they let her;
the one who takes home leftovers for next day's lunch.

One has been married for 40 years yet stayed herself.
Two stayed themselves and never married.
One married late and briefly,
the fifth early and long, freeing herself at last.
Two have grown children,
three have lived child-free. Five.

Well, it was five. One now lost—to youth, the irony
being that despite her age she was so young she rode
her motorbike to the final moment, doing what she loved.
Then there were four.
No one now takes cinnamon in her cappuccino.
There will be three someday, then two, then one.

That one will carry in herself some of the best of all of us
because in each other's presence some of the best
of each of us came forth. And when she goes,
the women we were to one another
will all wink out, the work we've shared
lasting perhaps a little while beyond us.

For now, we go on witnessing each other ride the current
out to sea, aware our time's not open ended.
We cling like lovers when we part, we say
I love you before hanging up the phone, and one
to one we all confide concerns about the others' health.
Laughter's astringency balances such tenderness.

But when young ones, unseasoned, condescend,
a voice in each of us hisses *Watch it, child. You have no clue*
who's living under this disguise; for if our true height
could be measured, you'd see how low we stoop for you,
how if we straightened we would wear
the clouds for garlands in our hair.

Needlework

A sewing basket of sorts: swatches, patches,
bits and scraps, post-it jottings, scribbles
in the margin of a grocery list—an overheard
remark that warrants remembering. Or images:
the incurled claw of a frozen finch
corpse in the garden. Sometimes just a word.
Or a newspaper clipping, brittle, yellowed.

This one, for instance, on the nameless sister
of the Pharaoh Kufu, he who built the Great
Pyramid. She disobeyed him, about what we don't
know. As punishment, he exiled her from royal burial
plans and sentenced her to a brothel. So she charged
each customer a stone for her favors, and this way
built her pyramid of a thousand vengeful stones.

Or these two remnants, scribbled notes from early
America: Deborah Franklin, common-law wife of Ben
for 37 years. She raised his child by another woman,
ran his printing press, wrote and edited his almanac, and
while he was in London trying to negotiate
a truce—yet finding time to do his own experiments—
back in the colonies, she died alone.

Deborah never met Sarah, wife of evangelical
theocrat Patrick Henry. She brought him as dowry
a Virginia plantation, small, with six enslaved persons.
He imprisoned her in the cellar for the rest of her life—
an alternative to the asylum, he claimed, since she suffered
from melancholia. Meanwhile, confident he'd done
God's will, he boasted, "Give me liberty or give me death."

Lives of such women, unlived, wait patiently to be
embroidered as they deserve. But if you rummage down
among the rags, you find the selvage of anger hemmed
long ago by those mourned only now by this stranger
to Kufu's sister, Deborah, Sarah, so many selves—
including the self who stitched together, before she died,
the old woman who survived to write this poem.

Meteor Shower

For Verlorena

The Perseids were dense that year,
with peak activity pre-dawn, as many as 100 streaks
of fire an hour. That summer I was in the city,
a great city proud that darkness
falls there only in small pools, the way light
falls elsewhere. But modern miracles spoil us
so I lay in bed, laptop beside me like a lover, watching
NASA kindly stream the streams live. I don't know
what's more astonishing: the meteor shower
or manner in which I viewed it. Or human relatives
watching the same website, texting from Mongolia
and Rio and Zaire:

When does it start?
Oh look!
Did you see that one?
It's dawn now where I am.
Where are you?
Oh look, look.
In the babel of languages they reached
through space to talk to someone on this planet
about wonder. One texted—I couldn't make this up—
in Klingon. And someone answered, too.
I sipped my tea and watched. And
then of course I thought of you.

It was the Leonids, not the Perseids,
because it was November,
and you were busy tidying up to die.
After an impassioned life engaged
with the world, traveling the globe but loving
small places, telling stories of village women;
after that lifetime of politics and action
the ovarian cancer bloomed overnight.
You used those estimated six months well,
finished a book we got to help see print. Then you
asked me to come for a weekend, and I went
to Maryland to say we both knew my goodbye.

You were beautiful as always, tall, elegant, mature
as an empress, your long red hair bound unruly up,
wisps flirting to be tucked at, your wit and laugh
a piccolo and jazz bass in duet. You'd already told me
you were planning to check out soon,
not wait for the 'tackiness' as you put it. You already had
the stuff —and sure enough, I spied it in the fridge.
I was helping you cook me dinner as you insisted
(you had no stomach, only a tube strung from a vein
to a portable bag you wore like a fanny pack, with flair).
You were at the stove—always a proud, superb cook—
and asked me to get you something from the fridge.

And I saw it.
The large plastic container at the back of the shelf,
the cocktail you had somehow scored,
the two gallon tupperware jar of death.
You insisted I eat, and drink wine, for your vicarious
thrills, you said. So I chewed and swallowed and we
talked death and politics. The towers had fallen
two months earlier, drumbeats of war were full volume.
We sat helpless, two lifetimes—one almost over—spent
working toward peace, and talked death and talked politics.
Well, I'm sure leaving you with one hell of a mess, eh?
you said, then added softly, *I don't envy you.*

Then it was time for my proposal: that we get up
at 4 AM for the Leonids. After complaining
I didn't know how to coddle a dying woman,
you admitted excitement. You'd be up anyway, reading,
and you'd never seen a meteor shower, so just in time.
You lived on a dark street in a countrified suburb
with a clear view of the sky. We said goodnight.
I set my watch alarm and woke to see your bedroom door
across the hall ajar, a wedge of light on the floor. We
made tea, took mugs and blankets, shuffled through autumn
leaves to rickety garden loungers, settled in. It was warm
for November. We talked about the last time we'd stayed up

all night, manic on coffee and cigarettes, writing some
conference statement, remember? Talked about old lovers,
and how you missed Mali of all the places you had been,
and our grown children, and the memoir you'd so wanted
to write and now never would. *It is what it is,*
you sighed. You went over your plans:
You'd have the children come. You'd cook
a magnificent Malian feast and eat and drink by god—
because there wouldn't be time to suffer after-effects.
You'd see each child separately,
then cluster them together in your bedroom
and get royally stoned on grass.

Then you yourself would switch the tube
from nourishment bag to tupperware jar.
*I'll wear my favorite dress, from Mali, bold red,
embroidered with tiny mirrors.* We talked on, as
the heavens began to rain a splendor of dark energy,
slits of fire in the night scrim of space.
Once, I made more tea and wrapped
your blankets tighter while you joked I was trying
to give you pneumonia, ovarian cancer wasn't enough.
But you wouldn't go in. Finally, we sat in silence, rapt,
while glory streaked above us, needles of light
stitching downward, fast now, flakes in a blizzard.

That's us, too, you murmured. *Falling?* I asked. *Exactly.*
Some of us trying to leave that trail of light as we fall.
Only with darkness bleaching
toward dawn did we go inside to sleep a few hours.
Then I made coffee and you said
Oh god let me smell it, and grinned.
You showed me the dress. I praised your perfect taste.
The cab for the airport came.
We embraced, laughing and crying. You said *Write as much*
as you goddamned can as long as you can, adding
You brought me a peak activity. A literal one.
Thank you for the Leonids.

Three weeks later your son called to tell me.
The feast, the red dress, how stoned they'd gotten
and how much they'd laughed, and how, after
you'd switched the tube, you lay back looking
radiant and said *I love you.* Then, reporting back
to the last, said, *Ah. I can taste it.* And smiled. And slept.
Dark matter is ninety percent of the known Universe,
meaning it's what we don't know.
Dark energy moves stars, blows solar winds.
and we've never known what it is. We are dark
to each other and our selves are dark to us,
ourselves of whom we are ignorant

that each of us is every second
in the act of falling, sailing through darkness
for such a long time we forget light
until some atmosphere we encounter
sets our small lives briefly aflame.
So I lay in my bed, knowing nothing,
propped on my pillow watching the Perseids
fade like my memories of you, us,
two among many, traveling for such a short time
ignorant of what we are: unknown dark matter
moved by unknown dark energy to become
light as we fall, only then.

Final Proof

The old woman sits in her garden, chilled
balloon-glass of Sancerre in one hand, joint
in the other, content. Late afternoon light
lies low, pale gold as her wine. The jays stop
screeching, the cardinals take over. The old
woman has just showered after hours of work
in the mud, cleaning sludge from the waterfall's pool,
rewiring the pump, draining, washing, refilling

the pool with clean water glittering clear in the sun.
She has scrubbed and filled the birdbaths, pruned the
grapevine, tried again to teach the wisteria its proper place.
She has treated one rose for fungus, another for aphids,
hosed down the slate, and oiled the table and chairs.
She has put in the annuals: pansies, violas, herbs, salad bed:
lettuces, spinach, chard, sorrel, arugula, kale.
Now she sits, the cool of a white linen

shirt on her skin, conscious of all the ways she's content.
Running fingers through her hair, still damp-ringleted
from a shower, she savors her soap-smelling flesh,
the fresh linen, the light, the beauty of this garden
she herself this same old woman planted, back
when she already was not-young. (But not-young is different
from old.) All day she has thought blissfully of nothing but what her
hands do. Now she feels sexy. It's true.

Her muscles scream from work but the pain reassures
her she at least has them. The waterfall, plashing softly,
is romantic. So (the old woman recalls) is she.
An impulse! Perhaps phone that special old lover?
But all I'd really want to say, she knows, is
I was thinking about you. Just that.
And there would be no way of leaving
it at that, it would become An Issue.

The old woman has finally learned some things,
among them that her energy and time grow short,
and art's more faithful than most lovers. So, instead, she sips
her wine and writes a poem. This one, in fact. No fool,
however, she relies on morning's glare, content to be severe
on content and on form then. First drafts as fragrant
as a tipsy garden poem you cut to bring indoors—in fact,
first drafts of any kind, including love—she now ignores.

III.
Grey Matter

No Signs of Struggle

Growing small requires enormity of will:
just sitting still in the doctor's waiting room
watching the future shuffle in and out,
stooped; watching it stare at you
while you try not to look. Rare is an exchange:
a smile of brief, wry recognition.

You are the new kid on the block. Everyone here
was you once. You are still learning
that growing small requires a largeness
of spirit you can't fit into yet: acceptance of
irritating help from those who love you; a giving
way and over, but not up. You've swallowed

hard the contents of the "Drink Me" bottle, and felt
yourself shrink. Now, familiar furniture looms,
floors tilt, and doorknobs yield only when wrestled
round with both hands. It demands colossal patience,
all this growing small: your diminished sleep at night,
your handwriting, your voice, your height.

You are more the incredible shrinking woman
than the Buddhist mystic, serene, making do
with less. Less is not always more. Yet
in this emptying space, space glimmers,
becoming visible. Here is a place
behind the eyes of those accustomed

to what some would call diminishment.
It is a place of merciless poetry, a gift of presence
previously ignored, drowned in the daily clutter.
Here every gesture needs intention, is alive
with consciousness. Nothing is automatic.
You can spot it in the provocation of a button,

an arm poking at a sleeve, a balancing act
at a night-time curb while negotiating the dark.
Feats of such modest valor, who would suspect
them to be exercises in an intimate, fierce discipline,
a metaphysics of being relentlessly aware?
Such understated power is here, in these

tottering dancers who exert stupendous effort
on tasks most view as insignificant. Such quiet beauty
here, in these, my soft-voiced, stiff-limbed people;
such resolve masked by each placid face.
There is immensity required in growing small,
so bent on such unbending grace.

Grey Matter

1. Movement Disorder

Given decades of picketing, petitions, a jail or two,
and worse—the torture of meetings—I find
the diagnosis name hilarious.

It's all in the grey matter—slang for the brain—deepening
to dark matter. But no one's specified which shade of grey
I have: pearl? charcoal? Slang's not scientific, anyway.

What's scientific is a neurological disorder
they call degenerative (sounds like a moral judgment)
which prompts my lovely brain to spit

stutters through nerves and muscles so a lascivious dybbuk
hip hops along my fingers, pokes me in the eye,
spills coffee in my lap, trips me up, dresses me down,

skids my cursor across the computer screen, and cramps
my signature—the bold, flowing hand I was so vain about—
down to a drunken spider's web.

Ironic, to find myself ajerk, just when
I was discovering the value of being still. So, Brain,
what do we do now, you and I? You know

damned well you always were my favorite,
you know I never fell for that trash about having guts
or the heart as the seat of emotion. You know I knew

it was always you, neurotransmitters abuzz; electro-chemical
synapses; waves and frequencies jigging: oh splendid powers
of the brain, I always loved you best. Have I deserved this? No,

that's not scientific, either. Also absurd. Who deserves anything?
Recursive thinking—brain mulling on brain—can make one dizzy,
even someone apolitical, lacking movement disorders.

Well, Brain, as you fire ideas through these fingertips on keys,
I echo your vow: We'll go through this together, quarreling
lovers. But I ask three favors as we do—for both our sakes.

In the midst of shuddering, save us a place for stillness.
In the darkening grey, save us a space for laughter.
In the ticking hours, save us a time to make poems.

2. On Donating My Brain to Science

Not a problem. Skip over all the pages reassuring
religious people. Already a universal donor: kidneys, corneas,
liver, lungs, tissues, heart, veins, whatever. Odd

that the modest brain never imagined its unique value
in research, maybe saving someone else from what it is
they're not quite sure I have. Flattering, that.

So fill in the forms,
drill through the answers,
trill out a blithe spirit.

And slice me, dice me,
spread me on your slides.
Find what I'm trying to tell you.

Earn me, learn me, scan me,
squint through your lens.
Uncover what I'd hint at if I could.

Be my guest, do your best, harvest me,
track the clues. This was a good brain while alive.
This was a brain that paid its dues.

So slice me, dice me, smear me on your slides,
stain me, explain me, drain me like a cup.
Share me, *hear* me:

I want to be used
I want to be used
I want to be used
up.

3. Images

No microscope sees what poetry can see,
images ghosting along dead nerve trails
leaving no evidence. Where

are they stored, the imagined, the remembered?
Some in the temporal lobe, most in the hippocampus—
but only while alive. Gone from lab slides.

What tells us how a brain
firing energy over light-years of a life,
glowing brighter until it begins to implode

flashburst—white maryjane shoes, grout in three brick steps,
a man smoking a pipe, a Bach fugue soaring steel-cable
incarnate up a bridge, a baby's cries "hut *laaa*! hut *laaa*!—

what tells us how a brain, concentrating itself,
densifying toward the event
horizon, can recall what only poetry records

flashburst—beach cabana-flap striped blue and white,
whiff of spring-rain soil, spasm of sex so pure it glistens,
birdchitter on awakening—what tells us

how such thoughts can live only under a poem's lens but vanish
even in the brain that documented them, as that brain burns
nova, scorching brighter and brighter until it cannot recognize

       flashburst—this sunflower-yellow-haired child
       splashing in a rain puddle, smiling,
       who holds my hand?

Uniquely Human

Only what I created after the illness constitutes my real self.
—HENRI MATISSE

That moment before. Before you and I learn
if Schrödinger's cat is alive in the box, before
the word is uttered that can't be taken back,
before the border's crossed, the phone rings,
the door slams. That moment when everything
is still conceivable, suspended, pre Big Bang,
before the first chord strikes, limiting all music.
Before it grows too late and ends too early.

I had imagined this, or something close
to this, so many times the diagnosis entered
softly, felt familiar. Why not me? Who gives a damn?
Not the Cat's Eye Nebula, so, really,
why should I? Except for being more curious
to see what I can make of this disease
than what it tries to make of me. For instance,
words to work poems with now, rarely used before:

Lurch. Stumble. Weave. Stagger. Fumble.
Stoop slowly so you don't pitch forward. *Tremble*
—though sure as hell before no living god—
jerk, spasm, freeze. You see? Actually, when macular
degeneration sent O'Keeffe, half-blind,
back to elementals, she wrote "Nothing
is less real than realism." So let's start
here: No other animal has this disease.

Its *symptoms* can be replicated in lab rats,
mice, monkeys, rabbits, but the illness,
in the words of one researcher, is, unlike
all others, "uniquely human." That
sort of statement gets a poet's attention.
So does this new finding: "The human brain refuses
to differentiate between imagination
and experience." Imagine that.

The sensory cortex reacts identically to
velvet, canvas, silk when fingertips touch
those textures and when eyes read the words
velvet, canvas, silk. Think of it.
(No, really. Think of it.)
The motor cortex lights up, too, when reading about
movement the same as when experiencing it.
I find the implications, I must say, staggering—

that the brain, one in a multiverse of brains,
mimics how light from suns gone nova millennia
ago still glows. Virtual reality is
a misnomer. All reality is virtual.
Meanwhile I, fearful only of feeling
wrongly unafraid, practice imagining
being alive in a world without color, taste, or smell,
unable to walk perhaps, or to speak clearly,

clearly unable to plant my sorrel seedlings
in rich spring dirt, or dice fresh garlic
into hissing olive oil, but human still—
if readiness is all, uniquely human.
Schrödinger, you see, also imagined entropy's
opposite: negentropy—the drive toward *forming.*
Negentropy is what will culture poetry from dying cells
till the imaginer, spent, becomes what is imagined.

So I can grant my bounded nutshell brain
infinite space to practice its insistence
on synesthesia, sensing no difference between
imagination and experience, stars' light
and suns long dead, the moment before the minute
after, and, traveling at the speed of thought,
the idea of how a hyacinth smells, the color
of dancing, the taste of this poem.

Looking on the Bright Side

A Light Verse Comfort

Living in an age of scientific agonists,
it's easy to forget there was a time
we'd have been burned alive.

True, they would have burned me
and my kind for so *many* reasons
so many times:
for loving a man while unwed,
for loving a woman,
for *being* a woman.
For being a woman who'd learned how to read.
For being a woman who knew how to write.
And this now, for trembling
with what must be surely possession
by Satan.

They're around still, the folks
who'd have burned us alive. How
they love burning things! Now
they set virtual fires to funding for research,
to laws that protect us when we can
no longer walk a straight line.

Which brings to mind a metaphor—what doesn't?—
about who we are really, all of us; what really happens
when we can no longer walk a straight line.

Navigating the night is hard enough
for species that rely on visual cues.
Easy enough when the moon is bright, but
what to do on moonless nights?

Well, the lowliest creatures, ones who
evoke our disgust, dung beetles,
they find their way.

These beetles roll balls of dung
for later use as, yes, food—or sometimes mating gifts.
Once they collect the dung, they quickly roll the ball
away from the pile, to avoid theft by other beetles.
They do this by moving in a straight line.

Scientists studying that behavior learned
the beetles could move in a straight line on moonlit nights
and on moonless nights, too—if light from the Milky Way
was visible. When the sky was overcast, or when the beetles
had tiny visors taped on to their heads to block their view
of the night sky, they wandered aimlessly.

This research is thought to be the first to document the use
of galactic light for orientation in the animal kingdom.

And I thought five thoughts:

1. Well, this too is science.
2. Is it possible to wander aimfully?
3. How *irritating* it must be to have a visor taped to one's
   tiny head.
4. So are we all, despite pretense of being human, dung beetles
   navigating the night by the flare of indifferent, celestial glory.
5. *Who needs to walk in a straight line, anyhow?*

At The Edge of The Wheatfield

The detailed focus on near objects may have reminded
the artist to concentrate on constant things in the world
around him, to avoid becoming ovewhelmed.

—PHILADELPHIA ART MUSEUM
2012 VAN GOGH UP CLOSE EXHIBIT,
FEATURING WORKS FROM 1886
UNTIL HIS DEATH IN AUVERS IN 1890.

What is constant in the world?
Fritillaries in a copper vase. A pair of boots,
scuffed, shaped by misshapen feet. A single iris.
Indolent grasses. Butterflies.
Four years to go, innocent of the date,
until stars will careen wheeling
across the night sky, crows will pepper the yolk
of noon, everything will change, move, overwhelm …

For now, try to act normal.
Try to earn money, be secure, independent.
Japanese prints are all the vogue.
Emulate them: their calm, stiff,
pastel shadows, their formal, flat
—*something is roiling beneath, rolling nearer*
in waves, something inside, something under,
four years to go—

Undergrowth, then. Back in fashion,
but in traditional style. Practice
your craft, drafting, discipline,
overwhelm fear at what *roils and writhes whirling*
beneath. Undergrowth. Yes. But tamed, tidy.
No, your palette knife slashes the sensible.
Your soil leaches power arching
up, twisting, *three years to go*

contorting each grass-blade to bend
under a wind unique to itself.
Undergrowth spreads from below,
from what cannot be seen from where
tree roots swivel their knuckles to grasp—
Trees, now, they're trendy. Allées. Poplars. Stately, serene,
magisterial. Troops in formation.
Try to act normal, paint trees.

But these branches and trunks gnarl, buckle,
snarled by a force overwhelming
straight lines, under the strain, the pressure
of growth. *Isn't that normal?* Perhaps,
but not popular. Overwhelmed
people choose not to live with such crippling
darkness on their smooth walls. Try
to act normal. There is no security, no independence

possible, only this pacing the edge of a field of
　　　Look! Look what breaks through! radiant wheat, lemon ears
　　　languid cranes dipping their long-necked arcs in a lagoon
a still life, then. Always reliable. Fruit in a bowl. Pastel
blossoms.　　*But look! sunflowers found in a gutter, brazen,*
coarse, angular—offending collectors.　　*Two years to go.*
Pears, then. Peaches, an apple. Stillness
at last. The bowl rests in quietude. Something to buy, hang,

hang onto … *but look at the air, at the space*
　　surrounding the fruit, encasing the bowl:
　　　hundreds of palette-knife scabs, thick, pulsing signals
　　that crackle the storm blowing nearer.　　*One year to go.*
No one can find normal, the straight line in nature
doesn't exist, life is not still, the canvas not flat,
because　　*something comes rolling in waves, seeping up*
　　　from *below*　　it will overwhelm stars to churn the night sky,

blackbirds to shadow midday, air to disrobe itself.
By the time a sole gunshot startles the crows
there will be no more waiting, no patience left. Time now
to enter the wheatfield enter yellows so bright
we still wince at their glare, blues bleak as black,
whites grey with exhaustion. Enter the energy
uncoiling inside your brain, watch more dimensions
warp into perspective, enter the screaming

color and torque they will call madness
but you will know as a health enter the force
that will drive hundreds of works those last
weeks: one masterpiece every day.
Welcome the whirlwind
let the storm break
over your head, break
through your heart
and let the rest go
so
  the rain
     pale curtain slanting
        young greens drenched ghost blue
           rinses off pain toward a loveliness
               past release now, past peace, at last
                    overwhelmed.

The Ghost Light

Lit from within is the sole secure way
to traverse dark matter. Some life forms—
certain mushrooms, snails, jellyfish, worms—
glow biolumescent, and people as well; we
emit infra-red light from our most lucent selves.
Our tragedy is we can't see it.

We see by reflection. We need biofluorescence
to show our true colors. Illumination can distort, though,
if external. When gravity bends light, huge galaxy
clusters can act as telescopes, elongating background
images of star systems to faint arcs—a lensing effect
like viewing distant street lamps through a glass of wine.

A glass of wine or two now makes me weave
as if acting a drunkard's part; as if, besotted
with unrequited love for the dynamic Turner
canvases spied out by the Hubble, I could lurch
down a city-street set without provoking
a crowd scene and every pedestrian walk-on stare.

Stare as long as you need to. If you think about it,
walking, even standing, is illogical—such tiny things,
feet!—especially when one's body is not *al dente*
any more. Besides, creature of extremes and excess,
I've always thought Apollo beautiful but boring,
a bit of a dumb blonde. Dionysians don't do balance.

Balance, in other words, has never been
my strong point. But I digress. More
and more these days, digression
seems the most direct route through
from where I've lost or found myself
out of place, mind, turn, time.

Place your foot just so, mind how you turn:
too swift a swivel can bring you down. Take your time
ushering the audience out, saying goodbye
to the actors. The ghost light
is what they call the single bulb hanging
above the bare stage in an empty theater.

In the empty theater of such a night, waking to meet
no external radiance, this is the final struggle left to win,
this the sole beacon to beckon the darkness in and let the rest
begin, this the lens through which at last to see both Self
and Other arrayed with the bright stain of original sin:
lit from within.

Bodily Knowledge

1.

The human brain weighs two percent of total body weight
yet eats 20 percent of the body's oxygen. Glymph and cerebrospinal
fluid remove the waste. The brain's waste.

Now what would that be? Regret?
"If only's"? "What might have been's"? "I wish I had's"?
Would it be petty grudges, chances lost, laziness, willful

ignorance? Or dreams, dream plots, dream
characters, the dross of a mind trying
to bring order to a brain, tidying up after

a hard day's thinking? Then again, there's evidence
that the brain's waste contains the thrill of cruelty:
neurons capable of composing a five-part fugue

aiming their creative impulse instead at rituals
that slice genitals, scarify skin, devise means to make
death welcome. Perhaps sins of omission, passivity,

constitute the brain's waste? More likely it's just
what gets forgotten, by chance or plan, an indifferent
blink in consciousness, a time-space shrug.

2.

But why did the brain invent ways to hurt the compliant
body? Its six types of joints—hinge, ball, socket, swivel,
gliding, saddle—all obey the brain. And what of

the three types of muscle: the skeletal
that pulls bones, the smooth that moves fluids, the cardiac
that pumps blood? They too—the first two—obey the brain.

The third does go its own way, outside the barrier
where the brain in its skull cell might plot caged revenge.
Why else serve this life sentence obsessing on blood

unless blood had a mind of its own? Because
all the while, a garnet current courses
60 thousand miles of veins in 60 seconds,

each drop flushing the rapids of the heart once
every minute. So preoccupied, blood has no time
to calculate our suffering, unconcerned as brain is

about who gets saved or killed. Until the known
universe dies, that is—when one's own
heart's blood and brain's waste are spilled.

Invitation

When you grieve for yourself—
not pity, you understand, but mourning—
it's not for old times or missed boats.
There's one reason only: you find you've lost
stillness. Well, not when asleep, you're still
when asleep. Then again, you're asleep, so can't
relish reflecting the peace of a mirror-like lake.
Awake, wind always ruffles your surfaces now.

It's a bit tiring, yet you'd best
get accustomed to it:
these small spasms that jerk you
about are mere samples,
the buzz of what's coming.
You can't be at peace outwardly,
anymore—the way you're at peace
in your depths now. Better that

than the reverse. Look, you're in sync:
universe, you, all life
metabolic, ceaseless in motion,
waves, seeds, eggs breaking
open galaxies wheeling,
colliding, suns dying ablaze
cells dividing who needs stillness?
Stillness is death.

No. Even death can't be still. Death's alive
with activity, bright putrefescent bacteria.
Compost squirms hot, catabolic.
Stillness not to be found since the big bang
shuddered awake through each vibrating string.
Who are you, then, to mourn? Whitman dared sing
the body electric. Here's your chance.
Go him one better, dear. *Dance.*

IV.
Dark Matter

A Worm of Robins

Not having died yet, I can't say
how difficult it is, or even if it is.
I'm sure it varies. Death must have
the widest repertoire of all, considering that
the universe's sole consistency is entropy.

But this I know so far: for me, at least,
likely it's not pain or fear or fear of pain
or life's small cruelties or monstrous ones
that can make dying hard. They'd make it easy,
I should think: to leave, to sleep, slip free.

But suddenly in autumn, morning glories
poke soft cerulean heads above the crisp
ivy they've climbed to the top of my garden fence.
Here. They swivel, seeking the pale November
sun. Three mornings later, they are done.

And suddenly in winter, bent double by a freezing
rain, hurrying along Ninth Street, *there*: swarming
a thorntree blistered with red berries, maybe thirty
robins. That's called a worm of robins, I discover.
Passers-by scold the soaked old woman who laughs,

leisurely taking pictures with her phone. *I'll* plant
a hawthorn! she thinks—but finds they live for centuries,
needing decades to fruit. Plant then for others, I learn,
hold your own brief hour in light regard. It's sweetness
that turns leaving sour, joy that makes dying hard.

The Young Artists at Rockwood Music Hall

They feel they are old, they are sure of it.
Like those people who think time is passing
them by all the while on the contrary time
stands or sits still at their side
as it does for each of us every moment
until it doesn't. They tune their instruments,
making ready, certain they are old.

And they are, for artists so young—days stuffed
with the urgent coin of survival, nights emptied
of all but relationships, the unfinished business
of families, death-battles with childhood ghosts
of these grown children still yearning to be seen
by dazed parents, everyone still feeling powerless,
everyone waiting for their lives to start.

And lovers unloving or loving too much
or not knowing how to love, or settling for habit
or trying, *trying* to do it differently, this time.
And children in some cases, adored and resented,
chosen but still displacing the artists
from what else they were making, their music.
Their music.

Their music alone knows what's coming.
Best to keep that from the musicians,
though one or two of them glimpses the secret, a shadow
cast by the blinding flare of elation, the making
of music. Look where it moves their bodies, transported,
look at their faces, free for this moment at least
from money fears, parents and lovers and children,

and old as they feel they are suddenly young
as they are. But it's over so soon.
The crowd whistles and claps and we gather around
the artists with ignorant praise. There is mention of going
for pizza. The old woman waits
a respectable interval and says early goodnights,
smiling, making her way to exit and street

and taxi, clutching her key to the safety
of bed. Yet it can't be held in
any longer, and in the dark cab,
speeding away from the young musicians,
the old woman weeps for them,
weeps for them,
weeps.

Trying to Write A Poem At the Very Last Minute

If readiness is all, then right now I am nothing.
In four hours I am due to offer some new work
at my monthly artists' group. Will I again present myself
alone, come empty-handed, commenting on others' art?
For shame. This is no writing block. I even blocked out
blank hours on the calendar. The world discovered that,

and ate them. That's how it's been, for the most part. Scribbling
in the corners of time, on airplane tray-tables, jotting notes
on scraps while the child napped, jolting down poems
on subway rides, voice messages left for me by me: a line,
an image, a single word, like "anamnesis"—loss of forgetfulness.
So I'll remember it. Remember who I am.

The world demands. Human suffering intercedes,
grief's eruptions interrupt, need pounds at the door, need
phones insistently, met by my hubris rising to heal
its wounds. These were my choices. I alone am to blame.
Livelihood takes its tolls, too, until I've measured
out my life in demitasse spoons. When did I marry the world,

start treating poetry like a backstreet lover, with secret rendez-vous,
the assumption of passion, hurried lovemaking's reliance on technique,
fantasies of the next time having more time together? When did
the world, taking me for granted, heave itself husbandly over
in bed, belching and farting, wanting sex and a snack and a backrub
and loyalty, all at once always nonstop and right now?

Friends cluck in comfort, "But look what you *have* done"—
meaning don't do what they haven't. Some urge, "Take a break,"
—meaning, see *them*. Interruptions themselves get adjourned
by intrusions, disrupted in turn by suspensions. There's no way back.
Crows ate the breadcrumbs, and the night's coming on. I see them
sometimes, scrawled in pale flame against the 2 AM blueblack page:

all the lost poems, unwritten, half-finished, souls damned
before birth, ghosts of lives unlived, dancing
in Limbo's windless silence, haunting their betrayer.
I have never sat long enough, still enough, mute enough,
for enough poems to unleave themselves, break open,
and bloom. Then again, who has? Where is "enough"?

This here, right here, is a clever conceit, some light verse growing
darker each stanza. But it's something to offer the artists, something
to conjure with at the least, at the last, at the very last minute,
smoke, mirrors, technique, while the passionate promise
—different, next month!—is pierced through my heart by the arrow
of time, shot from a too-slack-strung bow. The very last minute was
now.

The Excavation

National Geographic Society announcement, June 2006:
*The 1600-year-old mummified remains of a young adult were covered
with red pigment and bear tattoos, and her imposing tomb signified
high status. It was discovered 400 miles northwest of Lima, Peru, near
the summit of the pyramid Huaca Cao Viejo, a sacred site in Moche
culture, which flourished well before the rise of the Incas. Among
the burial trove—gold, fine textiles, semiprecious stones, weaving
materials and needles befitting a woman—lay two ceremonial war
clubs and 28 spear throwers, items found never at women's grave sites
but exclusively in tombs of Moche men. Nearby lay the skeleton of
another, smaller woman dead from apparent strangulation, a hemp
rope still around her neck. It was the rope, via radiocarbon analysis,
that dated the burial of both women to approximately* CE *450.*

I.

You are here, I know it. Where?
Come to me. I command you.
If I could see through this fog! I wander
and wait, calling out for you, Little One
of my Choosing, culled from the herd,
where are you? Come! I demand you!

You were mine the moment I saw you,
plucked you from filth to be granted my favor,
raised high by me, brought to the Great House.
How hard you struggled—so small,
but you kicked, spat, hit,
scratched, screamed—and I laughed

while they scrubbed you and wrapped you in silks,
laughed as you gorged on roast pigeon and mangos,
laughed as you cowered and glared at me.
You are near, I feel it. I command you to come
to me. I know you can hear me even through
this thick fog. Useless to fight me, you know it.

I always was different, stronger than all
of my brothers, my father's true son, though
a woman. I set my mind and my teeth on it,
refusing to be female, not-man, less than human.
I was more than human, I knew it.
When the Others came from the north,

it was I who led the Moche into battle. I
cut down our enemies, laughed at their screams,
killed and killed until none were left.
My arms ached with killing. My enemies, my own
kind, both saw me then with wonder,
a woman of power, freak or demon.

I would be neither. I would be a god. From that day,
men would fear me, women revere me,
and all would worship me. I wore the condor-
feathered cloak. There was a price.
I was the object of their adoration,
not their love. How can the devout imagine

the unspeakable loneliness of their god?
Then, one day, I was hunting, and there it
was, hiding, squatting in its fetid hut,
a creature of huge eyes and rags. You
would come to love serving the god, though.
You alone loved the *me* in the god.

You watched when I bedded the man in the ritual,
then killed him once my belly swelled with my daughter,
the next god of war. When I fell, convulsing,
the last sight I saw was you bent above, weeping
for me as I died a hero's death. Why now are you silent?
You are here, you must be, I left orders for it.

You know I cannot be alone with these weapons that slew
so many—tools I used to prove I was human—more—
I was god. That was the price. You were the gift.

II.

You are here, I fear you will loom up
out of the fog as you did the day you seized me
by my hair in the corner of the hut by the meadow.
I had known seven summers. You took me
at seven summers only. You laughed. My father
groveled in gladness that I would be a slave

to She who was both man and god. There would be food
now, beer, gold, eager husbands for my sisters, an adobe
house, a private mound for when my parents died.
"You will be raised high," my mother said.
I knew nothing. Only fear and loss. I would need
to forget fear and loss if I wanted to live.

But I wanted to die. Though never enough. So I lived,
the god's favorite, crouched where you placed me.
At your feet as you sentenced captives to death.
At your table, tasting each dish for poison.
Beside your nightmares each night before battle.
Beneath your bed linen. Between your thighs.

You stank of blood and spices. Your voice softened
at my name. Naked, I smiled and danced for you,
I stripped off your armor. I bathed your scars,
some thick as rope. Once, after you'd slain twenty men
—in a single day, they said—I held the basin
while you vomited. I almost loved you then.

And when you fell I wept. It was so ordinary, like any
woman's dying, no spear in hand, no war cry in the throat.
But then I joyed in it—I joyed that it was over and each of us
was free. Until that night, when I remembered
that your end would mean my own, to serve you
through the afterworlds, raised high in death.

I ran. I ran, such terror in my mouth I can still
taste it like the poison I had planned to slip you
after tasting your food someday, but never had.
Of course your priests and mourners caught me,
dragged me as they had when I was seven,
shrieking, fighting, to the tomb where you lay

swaddled in gold armor plates, encircled by
your weapons and my weaving. Freedom would be
forgetting fear, but I turned fear to hatred long ago.
Now I must find new afterworlds to walk alone, as your calls
echo through the space that yawns between us.
I never loved you—though I could have. That last

ensnarement beguiles me still, a slave's desire
to speak to you, to make you understand. Except
for this: that day inside your tomb they forced
my face toward yours. I saw you stare at death
through inset turquoise eyes. I felt the rope fall, heavy,
on my shoulders, then tighten round my throat.

I sipped one final breath, knowing the last
sight I would ever see would be your face,
beautiful, severe, not seeing me.

III.

Letter home from student interning at the Huaca Cao Viejo dig:

*The local Indians are so superstitious! They shake their heads and
warn us that when you disturb a tomb, the so called "spirits" rise and
wander. They won't say whose spirits, though. This lady, wow. What
do you think? A queen? The wife or daughter of a military chief?
Can't be some mythic Amazon! We might never know. The professor
says she might've been pregnant, maybe died of something called
eclampsia, like convulsions. But he can't tell till there's a full lab
analysis, which could take years. And the second woman? Might have
been a suicide. I think they were lovers and she was in despair over
the queen's death. It's so romantic! But the professor thinks she was a
sacrifice. That would follow the common practice of ancient Andean
peoples. They made a ritual offering of a virgin to the spirit of a high-
born person during their funeral rites. Glad I wasn't around then!
He also says it's absurd to imagine that the women were lovers, and
extremely unlikely they ever even met, much less knew each other.
But the rope! How great is the rope? What a stroke of luck in dating
the find!*

Disclosure

A young musician's songs about the cruelty
of an old love sent you flying, to your surprise,
on a trapeze high beneath your dreams,
through the release and catch of your own
now-decades-dead desire. Hard to believe after so long
that grip has suffered so little loosening.
It was a minor grief, no genocide, no earthquake,
merely a broken start. Everyone told you so.

But after you stand in the middle of the room
a vigilant ringmaster, long enough;
after you learn it will circle around you
for years, adapting its path to circumvent
your whip, after you realize your scar
tissue from its claws is as close to healing
as you're going to get, you come to comprehend how
what was temporary is permanent after all.

Closure is a word that has no meaning.
But time and space do, they approximate distance.
Besides, life crowds out anything only half-alive.
Flesh does tire, and passion lessens. Soon,
you expect, you'll get to give up juggling.
Finally, you glimpse the trick: your memories
die when you do, not before—unless you turn
childlike, speechless, sucking cotton candy,

awestruck at the circus your life's become,
at the normality of freaks, clowns, and the wild
animal perched sullen on a tiny stool, at how
what was permanent is temporary after all.
Still, you are not ever safe from love's cruel melodies
however sweetly the young musician sings.
There can be no such thing as closure.
When you prod the beast, it springs.

Reading the Bones

for MN

I glimpse lines crazing my face in the windowglass,
crone's bones emerging. My eyes are growing larger;
soon they will perch on stalks and swivel, crustacean.
The better to see how others do it:
this last chance at living.

I watch them, agnostics entangled in their roots:
Jews reclaimed by feminist seders; African Americans
by Sunday church. The atheists study history, showing
a sudden personal interest in the past as they prepare
to enter it. As for the ones who've left already, they
and we, the dead and living, share mutual disbelief.

The message is we're too fatigued to change the myths
of ourselves at this stage, preferring to die, unmake
the world, in the familiar. Understandable. Yet I persist
in lusting to be seamless with the universe while still aware
of it—so I suspect a future darkly bright, kaleidoscopic
as symmetries glittering beneath eyelids rubbed dry of tears.

Time intimate as an embalmer. Deep Time. A passion
there so vast it flows inseparable from indifference, unlike
any passions I have known. Not those of youth, when I longed
to read the bones, thinking I knew the cost of such literacy.
Not zeal to save the world. Not desire in a lover
with the heat-seeking lips of a blood python.

No, this fire burns as ice, melts only for metaphors
that puzzle into patterns not of meaning but of beauty,
not of beauty but of till-that-moment the unthinkable.
For instance, retreating from Russia's winter, Napoleon saw
they had stuffed the broken windows of hospitals
with their frozen dead—feet, limbs, heads—to fit the apertures.

Decades ago, in Rome's Capuchin catacombs, I took notes
to play with in my private funeral games, then dared not
use them until now. Now they remind me that such crypts
are not to be confused with Phnom Penh's neat pyramids of skulls,
the tidy skeletons stacked in Vukovar, remains beyond wounded
at Wounded Knee, or Kigali's ossuary pits.

These catacombs are galleries for works of art. The medium
is human bone, room after small room, layered in the thousands.
Rosettes of sacrum framed by vertebrae. Jawbone
maxillae as vaulted triangles. Garlands woven of ribs
and carpals, arches of crossed femurs, roses tiled
with shoulder scapula and kneecap patella.

No inch of cornice, wall, or ceiling is left unskulled. Smiles
of these fragmented, nameless dead form wallpaper
against which featured exhibits are displayed: the eight-pointed
star of foot phalanges, the winged skull flanked by a sacrum.
A boss of pelvises. An hourglass. Metatarsal flowers, tibia stars—
the full palette is used, all 206 bones of the human body.

And in the foreground, the named dead lie whole
and mummified on cushions plumped with bone.
Capuchin monks full-robed, a doctor who died ministering to
victims of the plague, elaborately shrouded nieces of a pope,
and, postured dancing, naked, the skeletons of three
small children. Breath catches suddenly. The air is dusty.

Another tourist, a priest, claims this artistry by friars done
in waves across centuries was to celebrate the resurrection.
Considering their chosen medium, I doubt that motive,
although John Donne did wrap himself in a winding sheet
while burning candles in the human skull he kept on his desk
as he wrote the devotions called the Holy Sonnets.

His own devotion, however, he reserved for poetry. I too
have a skull above my desk, a photograph of the shape
formed by rose petals, delicate, dissonant. Each day I pay
respect to death. Respect was simpler, I admit, when death was
an abstraction. Now, friends in the ICU need visits,
and entrust me with defending their DNR directives.

So here's another lament for the makers: Muriel, Dorothy, Florika,
Simone, Eve, Pauli, June, Carolyn, Audre, Bella, Barbara, Andrea,
Wilma, Adrienne, Grace, Gerda, Mary, Lesley, Koryne, Kate ...
naming my dead, the women who made mischief, poems, laws,
pies, incremental seismic change. All the arguments, the laughter,
the suffering, silenced now. Whoever's next, I'm done with eulogies.

Nevertheless, I understand more deeply than I would prefer
why those obsessive friars, assured by the reliable supply
of their materials, built that world. Don't you and I
construct our days using what we drag back from nights

spent foraging our losses? What other materials
does anyone ever really have? The catacombs are everywhere.

Look! Do you see? A rose, a star! The hourglass fills,
drains. Ignore the tourists, look away from the window.
Here, wear the garland; it's meant for you. So are these
fragments, assembled with passion, indifference, reliable pain.
Look! Do you see? A poem, layer on layer, words puzzled together,
bones from the catacomb of a brain.

This Dark Hour

Late summer, 4 AM. The rain slows to a stop,
dripping still from the broad leaves of blue
hostas unseen in the garden's dark.
Barefoot, careful on the slick slate slabs,
I need no light, I know the way,
stoop by the mint bed, scoop a fistful

of moist earth, then grope for a chair,
spread a shawl, and sit, breathing in the wet green
August air. This is the small, still hour
before the newspaper lands in the vestibule
like a grenade, the phone shrills,
the computer screen blinks and glares awake.

There is this hour: poem in my head, soil in my hand:
unnamable fullness. This hour, when blood
of my blood bone of bone, child grown to manhood
now—stranger, intimate, not distant but apart—
lies safe, off dreaming melodies while love sleeps, safe,
in his arms. To have come to this place, lived

to this moment: immeasurable lightness.
The density of black starts to blur umber. Tentative,
a cardinal's coloratura, then the mourning dove's elegy.
Sable glimmers toward grey; objects emerge, trailing
shadows; night ages toward day. The city stirs.
There will be other dawns, nights, gaudy noons. Likely,

I'll lose my way. There will be stumbling, falling, cursing
the dark. Whatever comes, there was this hour when nothing
mattered, all was unbearably dear. And when I'm done
with daylights, should those who loved me grieve
too long a while, let them remember that I had this hour—
this dark perfect hour—and smile.

Disappear

It will be harder than expected, less severe
than dreamt. Bait your language to snare
particles and constellations. They won't care.

Plan to close with an epic song, naming the sheer
grace of galaxies, quarks, mitochondria, each atmosphere
you've loved, every breath, everyone, everywhere—

a youth-burdened goal: greedy, assured, unaware.
Rather wring joy from whatever the tide can spare:
a shell's opaline luster, the sway and creak of a pier

that moors nothing, how driftwood arms uprear
along the time-swept vastness of a winter heart, austere
as mercy, pointing in all directions to no there.

We are born screaming, cradled by the bier.
Why not go gentle into that goodnight, then? Why glare
with rage? Pity the drunken poet's fear,

shrug off his bombast. Opt for a quiet tone, wry tear;
invoke laughter, step lightly, be of good cheer.
Live at the ready. Sacred each passing year

within grasp beyond reach, unknowably clear,
until all you were, crashing against the shallows of here
as pearls of foam, ebbs, and you just

Other poetry titles available from Spinifex Press

Lupa and Lamb

Susan Hawthorne

> wind fills my ears with such stillness
> all I can do is listen
> to the echoing spill of the unheard

This collection of imagist poems combines mythology, archaeology
and translation, drawing on the history and prehistory of Rome and
its neighbours to explore how the past is remembered. Under the
guidance of Curatrix and Sulpicia, travellers Diana and Agnese are
led through the mythic archives, taking the readers with them.

"The talk's torrential, the company countless, the cultural crossovers
dizzying. Expect the unexpected."

— Judith Rodriguez AM

ISBN 9781742199245

The Abbotsford Mysteries

Patricia Sykes

> As if we fit together like old shards
> *orphan, unfortunate, drunk, prostitute*
> in a neat history of broken glass

The Abbotsford Mysteries incorporates a medley of voices and experiences, drawn from the archives of the Abbotsford Convent, the memories of poet Patricia Sykes and her sisters, and the oral memoirs of over seventy other women. Together their voices come alive in the poems, creating multiple pathways through memory and time as they map and navigate their institutionalized lives.

"Spirited and fugitive, lively and resistant, the girls in these poems speak through a powerful blend of the lyrical and the verbatim in a bare, intense, even visionary form of 'writing back' — against and into history. These are moving, compassionate poems full of the motif of river: life, undercurrent, debris — and the deeply aspiring self."

— Philip Salom

ISBN 9781876756956

The Mad Poet's Tea Party

Sandy Jeffs

I live with schizophrenia
and all her moods
she is the housemate from hell

Sandy Jeffs shares her journey through madness over four decades, drawing inspiration from Lewis Carroll's *Alice in Wonderland* and the motley gathering of characters at the Mad Hatter's tea party. Delightful and insightful, playful and serious, witty and whimsical, *The Mad Poet's Tea Party* provides a devastating commentary on how society treats those with mental illness.

"Sandy Jeffs lives her art and opens up her unique soul to us. Her writing makes us laugh, enlightens us and moves us with her bewitching words. This book is a treasure and testament to her wonderful gift."

— Elena Kats-Chernin

ISBN 9781742199498

Accidents of Composition
Merlinda Bobis

> Sometimes, this is the story of writing:
> word not made flesh, but eternal stone.
> And we wear it around our necks,
> always the weight of what we have written.

The eyes catch a black bird close to an eerie sun. Instantly, a poem: an accident of composition. Award-winning author Merlinda Bobis returns to poetry with this collection of seventy-six poems that trace the accidents of art and life, taking us on a circumnavigation of the globe.

"These revelatory poems travel through marginal histories and colonial encounters with an abundance of courage, curiosity, clairvoyance and humanity. Bobis is a lyrical shapeshifter; her dramatic luminosity and narrative flourishes inhabit other worlds."

— Michelle Cahill

ISBN 9781742199986

Feminist Fables

Suniti Namjoshi

> There was once a man who thought he could do anything, even be a woman. So he acquired a baby, changed its diapers and fed the damn thing three times a night. He did all the housework, was deferential to men, and got worn out. But he had a brother, Jack Cleverfellow, who hired a wife and got it all done.

Suniti Namjoshi is elegant and subversive in creating new patterns of meaning through stories that are simultaneously spare and full of richness. An ingenious reworking of fairy tales from East and West.

"Suniti Namjoshi is an inspired fabulist."

—Marina Warner

ISBN: 9781875559190

If you would like to know more about Spinifex Press
write for a free catalogue or visit our website.

Spinifex Press
PO Box 105
Mission Beach Queensland 4852
Australia

Orders:
PO Box 5270
North Geelong Victoria 3215
Australia

www.spinifexpress.com.au
women@spinifexpress.com.au